ASPECTS OF P.E.

SPORT IN SOCIETY

Kirk Bizley

Heinemann
LIBRARY

To the memory of my dear father

First published in Great Britain by Heinemann Library
Halley Court, Jordan Hill, Oxford OX2 8EJ
a division of Reed Educational & Professional Publishing Ltd

Heinemann is a registered trademark of Reed Educational & Professional Publishing Limited.

OXFORD FLORENCE PRAGUE MADRID ATHENS
MELBOURNE AUCKLAND KUALA LUMPUR SINGAPORE TOKYO
IBADAN NAIROBI KAMPALA JOHANNESBURG GABORONE
PORTSMOUTH NH (USA) CHICAGO MEXICO CITY SAO PAULO

© Reed Educational and Professional Publishing Ltd 1997

Designed by Celia Floyd
Printed and bound in Italy by L.E.G.O.

01 00 99 98 97
10 9 8 7 6 5 4 3 2 1

ISBN 0 431 07488 7

British Library Cataloguing in Publication Data

Bizley, Kirk
    Sport in society. – (Aspects of P.E.)
    1. Sports – Social aspects
    I. Title
    306.4'83

Acknowledgements

The Publishers would like to thank the following for permission to reproduce photographs:
Action Plus Photography p30; Action Plus/Glyn Kirk p43; Action Plus/Neil Tingle p36;
Action Plus/Richard Francis p45; Allsport p18; ASP/George Herringshaw p28; Associated Press
p37; Barnaby's Picture Library p38; Camera Press/John Evans p34; Coloursport/Andrew
Cowie p40; Empics/Neil Simpson p42; Empics/Ross Kinnaird p19; Empics/Tony Marshall
p16; Hulton Deutsch pp7, 21, 22; Hulton Getty p6; Image Bank p24; Michael Cole pp17, 41,
44; Mike Brett Photography p23; Patrick Eager Photography p15; Robert Harding Picture
Library p13; Robert Harding Picture Library/A Tovy p5; Science Photo Library/Krassovsky
p27; Trinity Newspapers p20

Cover photograph reproduced with permission of Empics Sports Agency / Michael Steele.

Our thanks to Nuala Mullan and Doug Neate for their comments in the preparation of
this book.

Every effort has been made to contact copyright holders of any material reproduced in
this book. Any omissions will be rectified in subsequent printings if notice is given to
the Publisher.

Contents

Words in **bold** in text are explained in the glossary on page 46

1 The history of sport

Origins

As people become increasingly health-conscious, more and more of them are taking up sports and physical activities as an enjoyable way of spending their leisure time. Sport is seen as very important, not just by fitness-freaks but by very many ordinary people who enjoy relaxing in good company, doing something that brings many hidden benefits. In this book, you will look at many aspects of sport in society, but first, how did it all start?

Many of the techniques used in sport today had their origins in hunting, fighting and the general survival skills needed by our distant ancestors. In primitive cultures and early civilizations the fittest survived. Those who could throw spears accurately and powerfully, who could track, chase and catch food, and who were strong enough to fight against enemies were the ones who lived longest.

During those times there were no countries or nations as we know them, but people lived in groups as communities. From this, small settlements developed, then towns and cities, and eventually nations. As time went by, people saw the need to protect the communities they lived with. Gradually this led to the formation of armies. The regular training of their soldiers led in turn to the development of many sporting activities, especially combat sports.

Armies needed to be ready for battle. They also needed to be kept occupied and fit, and they achieved this through practice and training. Much of this involved an element of competition. Wrestling and boxing developed from these activities (the Olympic wrestling event is still known as Greco Roman wrestling) and many of the **martial arts** which are popular today also began at this time, in the East.

The first stadiums designed to stage these sports were built by the Romans. The events often involved men fighting against each other and against animals. It is interesting to note that the shape of these stadiums has not changed very much from Roman times until now, although the facilities are likely to be very different.

Much of the sport that went on in the Roman amphitheatres was very cruel and violent. It often involved animals or men fighting against each other to the death.

Fact File

Five thousand animals are recorded as being killed in one day in AD 80, in the amphitheatre, and there is a record of 400 bears and 300 lions being killed in one day during the reign of the emperor Nero.

Sporting contests evolved over the years and became more related to skill, strength and stamina. One of the first recorded gymnastic type activities occurred 3000 years ago in Crete (in the Minoan period) when young men and women used to perform bull dances. They would vault over the head of a bull, using the horns to grip onto the animal's back and then somersault off onto the ground behind them. This was almost certainly performed in front of spectators and was a most important ceremony.

Horses were also linked with sport very early on. As long ago as 1350 BC, horses were trained and used for war and combat, so it was essential to be able to ride well. From this, and chariot racing, the sports of horse racing and show jumping have evolved.

Contests between men also started many years ago. There are drawings on the walls of Egyptian tombs dating from 2300 BC which clearly show some wrestling techniques. Modern Olympic wrestling is very similar to what took place over 4000 years ago.

Fact File

ASPECTS OF P.E.

One of the most popular martial arts is judo, which dates in its present form from the late fifteenth century – not as ancient as is popularly believed. However, it probably had its roots in the activities of the Samurai warriors in Japan.

There is no doubt that sport in some form has existed in all cultures throughout the world for thousands of years. Cave paintings which are 20 000 years old that show hunters with basic weapons, also clearly show the movements made.

The Colosseum in Rome, where the ancient Romans held brutal competitions

Sport gets organized

Considering sporting contests and activities have been taking place for centuries, organized sport as such has developed relatively recently. It has its roots in the various types of combat, competition and festivals which went before.

The ancient Greek Olympics are probably the best-known and earliest example of organized sports. Several thousand years ago, the many states that made up Greece were almost constantly at war with each other. However, they would stop fighting at intervals to have a contest of athletics, wrestling and combat between contestants from the various states. This competition was held at the temple of Zeus, at Olympia. The first recorded contest took place in 776 BC and lasted for seven days.

The Olympian Games, as they were known, were one of four ancient games held by the Greeks. The others were the Isthmian, Pythian and Nemean games, but it was the Olympian games that generated the most interest. Envoys would be sent out early in the year to get all the contestants ready and prepared. There were even facilities made available for some of the contestants to prepare and train before the games. There was a ruling that the competitors had to train for a month before the start of the games and the whole event was treated very seriously. The winner of each event would receive an olive wreath as a prize. These winners were then looked after by their home cities, living lives of comparative luxury at public expense!

The ancient Romans also had a form of games dedicated to their gods, and these involved more brutal types of competition, including fights to the death.

An early Roman games underway

The marathon winner in the 1908 Olympic Games

The Greeks were responsible for the start of one very famous contest – the marathon. In 490 BC the Greek army defeated the Persians at a place called Marathon and a runner, called Pheidippides, ran from Marathon to Athens with the news. History says he collapsed and died of exhaustion just after he arrived. The marathon distance is now set at 42.195 km (26 miles 385 yards) because that is the distance over which the 1908 Olympic race was run. The actual distance from Marathon to Athens was about 35 km (22 miles) and later races were run over about 42 km (26 miles). The 1908 games required the runners to run an extra 195 metres so that they could finish opposite the Royal Box at the White City stadium. This has been the standard distance ever since.

Sporting contests have been held all over the world. There were many local customs associated with the events, some of which still take place today.

A form of football is recorded as being played as long ago as AD 1352. Villages competed against each other, and the aim was to get a ball from one village to the next. There were no particular rules and the 'game' was often so rough that it was not unheard of for people to be killed.

Various games played with balls, and with bats and balls, were played all over the world and parts of some games were copied, or adapted, to invent other games. The main reason that these games tended to be based locally was because there was no transport. It was not possible to play against anyone except neighbouring teams. It was quite unusual – and took a long time – for anyone to travel from one country to another. The people who went on the very first cricket tours overseas travelled by ship, and the journeys could take several weeks just to get to the host country, before any of the cricket matches even started.

As transport started to improve and sport became better organized, competitions between areas within countries and between countries could take place.

National and international sport was possible and this led to a need for the rules and regulations to be agreed and written down.

This in turn has led to national and international bodies being formed to regulate the huge amount of international sport that is played today. All of the sports, and the major sporting competitions, have governing bodies with overall responsibility for their own particular sports. This has not always been a trouble free system and some sports have rather a large number of organizations claiming to be in charge internationally. Boxing is perhaps the best example of this: there are now four different organizations which claim to have jurisdiction over the sport and they all have their own world championships. There seems to be enough interest and money in the sport to support all of these bodies, however, which shows how much sport has evolved over a comparatively short space of time.

How sports evolved

The development and histories of some of today's most popular sports are fascinating.

Athletics

This sport involves track and field events, which have their origins in the Greek games of over 4000 years ago. Field events include the high jump, long jump, pole vault and triple jump, as well as throwing events such as the discus, javelin, shot putt and hammer. Track events include all of the running events.

Many of the field events are clearly based on hunting skills (you could also include fighting skills if you consider the javelin) and the track events are straightforward tests of strength, speed, skill and stamina. All of them are tests of power. It is easy to see how athletics has developed and remained popular over the centuries.

Basketball

This game was invented in America in 1891 by Dr James Naismith, a professor of physical education at the University of Kansas. The game was originally played using peach baskets nailed to the walls at each end of the gymnasium, which gave the sport its name.

It is very unusual to be able to trace the origin of a game as accurately as we can for basketball. It is even possible to state the day on which the first game was ever played – 20 January 1892!

Netball

The game of netball was originally derived as an indoor version of basketball. However, netball is now mainly played outdoors and basketball is played indoors! Netball started in England in 1895, when a visiting American, Dr Toles, introduced basketball. The game was gradually modified to make it better suited to women, and netball emerged.

Baseball

Some people claim that baseball is a version of rounders, which was introduced into North America in the eighteenth century by the early settlers. Settlers from Europe arrived in North America in the seventeenth century and there is a very strong likelihood that they were the originators of the game. Others believe that it evolved from a variety of different games originating from stick and ball games that have been played since the early days of civilization.

There is evidence of these types of games being played in the ancient cultures of Greece, Persia and Egypt, and they became popular in Europe during the Middle Ages.

Many Americans, though, claim that the game was invented by Abner Doubleday in Cooperstown, New York in 1839. This is why the American baseball Hall of Fame is based there.

Cricket

Cricket bats have been found which date as far back as 1750. In 1774 the game was played with two stumps with a single bail between them. The third stump was added in 1776.

Records seem to show that the game has existed in some form since the thirteenth century. Thomas Lord founded the Marylebone Cricket Club (**MCC**) in 1787 and the cricket ground, Lords, is named after him. Originally, underarm bowling was used, but in 1864 full overarm bowling was allowed. Many other changes have been allowed since, but all have to be agreed by the MCC, which still sets all the rules of the game.

Cricket is one of the oldest international games. The first **test match** (international event between nations) was played between England and Australia in 1877, and an English side toured in Australia as early as 1861.

The introduction of the one-day game format into cricket, where there is a limited number of overs for each team and a match is decided in one

Fact File

Cricket is responsible for a famous sporting term. In the early days of the game a bowler would be given a top hat if he took three wickets in succession. This was the origin of the term **hat trick**.

day, has given the game a big boost internationally and made it more interesting for many of the spectators. In many countries the one-day games subsidize the more traditional five-day test matches as they are far more popular with the fans.

W G Grace born in 1848 was England's best cricketer in his day

Soccer

The ancient Chinese played what could be termed a version of soccer, kicking the severed head of a defeated enemy around the battle area. From these gruesome beginnings, soccer has evolved to its present form and has become one of the most popular sports in the world.

The Football Association (**FA**) was formed in England in 1863, when it started to work out the agreed rules. Before long there was an organized administrative structure to run the game. The first international match took place between England and Scotland in 1872. The result was a goalless draw.

Professional soccer was allowed from 1885, which makes it one of the oldest professional sports in existence. The first FA Cup competition was held in 1871 and there were fifteen entries. The growth of the professional game led to soccer stadiums being built in many of the major cities in the UK. Most of the cities soon had at least one professional team and some (such as London) had more.

The **World Cup** was first organized in 1930 and was played in Uruguay. The host country went on to win the cup. The World Cup is now one of the major international sporting events. It was estimated that 2.7 billion television viewers watched the 1990 World Cup, which was played in Italy. The international organization which runs soccer (**FIFA**) has more than 160 nations affiliated to it and also runs the International Board, which considers and announces any rule changes which they think appropriate.

Rugby

In 1823, William Webb Ellis, a pupil at Rugby school in England, picked up a soccer ball during a game and ran with it. He is credited with starting the game of rugby football. The game took its name from the school where it was first played.

In 1895 there was an argument over whether players should be allowed to be paid to play rugby. This caused a split in the game. Rugby Union (played with 15 players on each side) was the **amateur** version of the game and Rugby League (with 13 players on each side) was the professional version. The two games are quite similar, although they are played to different rules. This rift between the two forms of the game lasted for 100 years, but in 1995, they sorted out their differences and Rugby Union players were allowed openly to earn money from the game. Up until then, there were very strict rules enforced by the Rugby Union ruling bodies – anyone who played Rugby League was banned for life from playing (or even being connected with) Rugby Union.

Rugby Union took longer than soccer to stage its own World Cup, which was held in 1987, and was won by New Zealand. The cup is called the William Webb Ellis Trophy, after the originator of the game, and is competed for every four years.

Tennis

Real tennis was played in the Middle Ages and **lawn tennis** (originally called 'tennis-on-the-lawn') started in the nineteenth century. Major Walter Clopton Wingfield, a British army officer, has been credited with inventing the game. There are also claims that it is based on an ancient Greek game called **sphairistike**, as were badminton and squash.

The first international championships for men were held in 1877, at the All England Lawn Tennis and Croquet Club in Wimbledon. The Wimbledon Championship is still recognized as the major championship today. In 1884 women were included as well.

There seems to be a very close link between tennis and squash. In the eighteenth century, inmates at Fleet prison used to hit a ball against the prison wall. In 1850, pupils at Harrow school used to practise against a wall whilst they waited to play rackets in an indoor court. They used a slow 'squashy' ball – and so the game of squash started to evolve.

Table tennis started as a game played between two students at Cambridge University, who used two cigar boxes and a champagne cork!

Hockey

There is evidence of hockey being played as long ago as 3 BC. The ancient Greeks, Egyptians and Romans played a version, and the games of **hurling** and **shinty**, both played in Ireland, are variations of it.

American Football

This version of football developed in the United States in the nineteenth century, and was based on soccer and rugby. The ancient Greeks had a similar game which was called **harpaston**, also based on getting a ball across a line, but in their version there was no limit to the number of players allowed on each team.

The first professional game was played in 1895 in Latrobe, Pennsylvania, but it was slow to take off as a major attraction. It was not until 1920 that the American Professional Football Association was formed, then the National Football League (**NFL**) was formed in 1922. The NFL is now one of the most powerful sporting bodies in the world. It controls the game in America and has been promoting it and establishing it internationally. The vital, final match called the **Superbowl** is the climax of the season and it has the biggest television audience of any of the major events.

Fact File

Of the ten most watched television programmes ever, the Superbowl features seven times.

The media, consisting of television, radio and the press now have enormous influence on modern sport, but with the exception of the press, this influence is fairly new. In fact satellite and cable television are still comparatively novel, having been available in the UK only during the last ten years.

Television

This is arguably the most powerful of all the media, especially since linked satellite networks have enabled programmes to be beamed live around the world. In the UK, sport on television has been regulated and controlled since the Television Act of 1954 – which shows how recent the growth of television has been. This Act gave the Government powers to draw up a list of protected events, known as **listed events**. These cannot be shown exclusively on **pay per view** channels (cable or satellite where you pay extra for the service). These listed events are shown on **terrestrial television** (TV stations which can be received in all homes, just using an aerial as a receiver). In 1991 the listed events were:

- home cricket **test matches** involving England

- the Derby horse race

- **FIFA World Cup** Finals

- the **FA** Cup final

- the Grand National horse race

- the Olympic Games

- the Wimbledon Tennis Championship finals

- the Scottish FA Cup final (in Scotland only).

The Commonwealth Games (when held in the UK), the Oxford and Cambridge Boat Race and all but the finals of Wimbledon were removed from an earlier list. Interestingly, of all the listed events only the Derby is covered by the independent TV networks (Channel 4); all of the rest are covered by the BBC.

These events are 'listed' to make sure that everyone who wants to watch what are regarded as the major sporting events can do so. As for other sports events, the governing bodies enter into quite long and complicated negotiations with the TV companies to decide who should televise them. The rights to broadcast are usually given to the highest bidders.

Most major events have extensive TV coverage

Terrestrial television

In the UK there are five television stations (BBC 1, BBC 2, ITV, Channel 4 and Channel 5) which are broadcast to every home. For many people, these are the only stations on which they can watch televised sport.

Television coverage of sport has been popular ever since transmissions first started in 1936. (The BBC had started in 1922 but it only broadcast on the radio.) Live coverage of sporting events soon became very popular, although many technological advances in cameras and transmitters were needed before all of this became possible.

Satellite TV is becoming more and more popular

Satellite and cable services

Sky launched its first Sky Sports channel on the Astra satellite in 1991 and it became available, by subscription, in 1992. In August 1994, a second Sky Sports channel was launched and in 1996 a third was added. A Eurosport channel is also broadcast by another satellite network, which means that satellite subscribers can now choose from four specialist sports channels which effectively broadcast sport 24 hours a day throughout the year.

It is a measure of its popularity that there are more stations dedicated to sport than to any other subject. There is also a lot of financial interest in sport.

In 1992, Sky obtained the rights to show live Premier League soccer, with their successful bid of £304 million. For this sum, it was allowed to transmit the games live on Sky Sports, and the BBC was allowed to show recorded highlights later. The ITV company had offered £262 million and had even fought against the satellite firms in the High Court, but they lost the case. This is a clear example of the governing body of a sport selling the right to broadcast their sport to the highest bidder. The football authorities knew that they were in an excellent bargaining position.

The cable and satellite companies rely heavily on sport as it makes up about half of their programme output. In 1994 they expected to show around 1300 hours of sport. The contrast to this is shown by the figures for ITV and Channel 4. On average each week, sports coverage makes up:

- 8 hours 28 minutes (5.88 per cent) on the ITV network
- 12 hours 52 minutes (9.24 per cent) on Channel 4.

Obviously the satellite companies are at an advantage because they can show uninterrupted coverage of events, no matter how long they last. They are able to devote the whole channel to sport, without worrying about transmitting other features.

There has also been a growth in 'pay per view' events where subscribers pay extra for special sporting events, notably boxing contests.

Television and sponsorship

The relationship between the TV companies and sponsors is very complex and controversial. In 1994, a government committee recommended that the BBC should stop broadcasting any sporting events sponsored by tobacco companies. The ITV network had already stopped this in 1987 and had its own Code of Programme Sponsorship, which clearly laid out what is – and what is not – acceptable sponsorship.

This was obviously identified as a sensitive area because all the guidelines have been very clearly set out. No news or current affairs programme may be sponsored but all – or part – of other programmes can be, provided general guidelines are followed. The main rules are that the sponsors must:

- not be allowed any undue influence
- be clearly identified at the beginning and end of the programme
- be manufacturers or suppliers of acceptable products.

Sponsors themselves like the coverage because it is a form of advertising for them and they can be assured of large audiences. Some of the highest viewing figures for any programmes in any year

are for sporting events. Sports sponsors can gain the additional benefit of being associated with something with a good, healthy image.

Fact File

For any one of the televised formula one Grand Prix races, the organizers can expect a worldwide audience of about 400 million. The sponsors who advertise on the cars could not obtain this sort of international publicity any other way. This is why they sponsor a team for up to £20 million a year. It is also often a way for them to get around some of the product bans imposed by TV companies.

Types of programmes broadcast

The many different ways in which television both shows and promotes sport include:

- live sporting action
- highlights programmes
- documentaries
- quiz programmes
- news bulletins
- information services (such as **Ceefax** and **Teletext**)
- coverage of major sporting events
- drama series
- sporting 'magazine' programmes.

One of the main reasons for the large and varied amount of sporting coverage is that sport is relatively cheap to televize. Many other programmes are far more expensive to produce and they do not have the uncertainty and drama which a live sports event can bring. In fact, sport is now one of the very few live programmes broadcast on any of the television networks.

It is clear that televised sport is very popular, with huge audience demand.

Benefits TV brings to sport

Television clearly benefits from showing sport but it does work both ways, since sport benefits through:

- **increased popularity** – many minority sports have increased in popularity, and boosted their numbers of participants, through TV coverage: for example gymnastics nearly always has a boom period immediately following an Olympic Games where there is extensive coverage

- **increased revenue** – income from sponsorship and endorsement of products can go directly to the sports or clubs

- **direct payments** – television has to pay for the rights to broadcast events and this is often one of the main sources of income for some of the governing bodies and their clubs.

A Question of Sport is the longest running UK television quiz programme

WILL CARLING   SALLY GUNNELL

Conflicts between TV and sport

Most of the time TV brings great benefits to sport, but there are some occasions when there are problems.

Seeing the game from every angle can be an unfair advantage

- Television may intrude upon an event – cameras, cables, commentators' positions, lights and sound crews can all get in the way of the spectators who have paid to come and watch. The TV companies want the best views for their crews but this could inconvenience the paying customers.

- Timings can be dictated by the TV companies and the audience may have to wait until the broadcast is ready to start. On some occasions the entire starting time of the event is decided by the TV companies. For an international event, the timing is often scheduled for the largest audience in one particular country – frequently the USA. This would mean a start in the early hours of the morning in Europe, to satisfy American viewers!

- The use of replays, both in slow motion and from various angles, can undermine the authority of officials, who do not have the benefit of these facilities. Many panellists and commentators can sit in judgement upon decisions. The TV companies demand that they can see all of the action from every angle and they have the technology to repeat the action very quickly – sometimes even on screens at the grounds.

- If particular sports are not covered on TV they may decline in popularity and participation in them may drop off. Television tends to concentrate on the major sports which attract the largest audiences, because this is what the sponsors and the advertisers want. Many popular games such as hockey and netball do not attract the same degree of TV coverage that soccer, rugby and cricket get.

- If a match or activity is shown live on TV, fewer spectators may go along to watch. This leads to a drop in revenue for clubs, who rely on the money they take from spectators. Therefore many of the sports organizations have arrangements to set aside some money which can be shared among all of the clubs, at the end of the season, so that they do not make financial losses.

- Televising one event live may encourage people to stay at home to watch, and not attend another sporting event or fixture. This means that a totally different sport could suffer!

However, despite all these factors, the benefits of televizing sport do appear to outweigh the disadvantages, otherwise it is unlikely that there would be so much sports coverage on television.

Technological developments are being made all the time, and television is constantly looking at ways of improving sports coverage. These include:

- small cameras being placed in the stumps to obtain close shots in cricket;

- formula one racing cars carrying cameras in their body work;

- officials using radio links to the TV directors and commentators, who can hear why certain decisions are taken.

Far more cameras – many remotely-controlled – are used to cover all aspects of the game. There are even plans for **digital compression**, a facility which will allow viewers to choose their own camera angles and be their own directors.

Radio

Most radio stations cover sport in much the same format as television. One of the main advantages radio has over TV is the large number of local stations that can cover local sport and teams. They do not have to rely on the big sporting events to attract listeners, as they can concentrate on any sport that is of local importance.

Obviously the radio stations don't broadcast pictures. Therefore they are not considered as rivals by the TV companies, and in particular the satellite companies. This means that they normally cover all of the major sporting events. Even the 'pay per view' events on TV are usually covered live by the radio stations. In fact they can even cover live events which

none of the TV companies are allowed to broadcast!

Some specialist radio stations concentrate largely or wholly on sports coverage. Radio 5 Live in the UK is a good example of this. It concentrates on news and sport, and its large output of live coverage includes sporting events such as athletics and major championships, as well as boxing, soccer and cricket. These radio stations can use satellite link-ups to cover sport from all over the world, and use the telephone networks to get the information broadcast.

All in all, radio does have some advantages over TV, such as:

- Broadcasting costs are much lower as only one commentator is needed (although sometimes they also have an expert analyst to add some comments), and the technology required to transmit the broadcast can be more basic than for TV.

- Radios are very cheap, they are portable and listeners can tune in when they are gardening or driving in their cars, so the potential audience is very large.

Radio sports commentators in action

The press

The press includes newspapers, magazines and books. All of these can be very influential and cover sport and sporting issues in a variety of ways.

Newspapers

All daily newspapers have sports sections, usually at the back, and some of them even have extra supplements for all the sporting news and results. Major sport often occurs at the weekends, when most people are free to watch sporting events. Therefore the Sunday papers usually offer very extensive sports coverage.

Press conferences are very common, where the press (and other areas of the media) have the opportunity to interview sporting personalities. These are not just the players themselves but include the managers and coaches. Many sports organizations insist that these press conferences take place. The press have the right to ask whoever they want to attend. Failure to do so can result in a fine or even a ban.

In many of the major American sports the players have a clause in their contracts which makes them available for interviews whenever requested. **Locker room interviews** (interviews with the players in the changing rooms immediately after the game) are very common as a result of this.

Newspapers are very influential as they publish the results, match reports, team news, rule changes and fixtures and they also comment on many major sporting issues and personalities.

After a series of poor results many newspapers were very critical of the then England soccer manager, Graham Taylor. There was a campaign to get him sacked, which was eventually successful, in 1993. There is little doubt that the extensive press coverage influenced this.

An England soccer press conference

Magazines

The number of specialist sporting magazines has increased rapidly in recent years. Most sports have at least one publication devoted to them. These magazines concentrate on issues to do with their sports, often printing very detailed information of interest to keen fans. Some of the major clubs even have their own fan magazines published. These are sold throughout the country, not just in the area where the team is based.

General sporting magazines are also proving popular and these look at all of the current issues in sport today. These magazines are usually printed monthly but there are some of them which come out weekly.

Books

Books related to sport fall into a number of categories, from novels to textbooks which deal with particular aspects of sport – much like this book! Some of the most controversial books of recent years have been **autobiographies** by famous sportspeople which have referred to incidents arising in their careers.

For many sporting personalities, writing a book is a way of earning extra money once their playing careers are at an end. It was also a way for **amateurs** to earn money without being thought of as **professional** performers.

Many other sporting personalities make a living from being **journalists** and writing for newspapers, as well as appearing on television commenting on the sport they have taken part in.

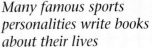

Many famous sports personalities write books about their lives

3 Amateurs and professionals

It is only comparatively recently that there has been any such thing as a **professional** sportsperson and only very recently that they have been paid such large amounts of money. Sometimes it is very difficult to tell the difference between a professional and an **amateur**, but there are definitions of what they should be.

An amateur sports match in progress

- **Amateurs** take part in sport, or an activity, as a pastime or a hobby rather than for financial gain. They take part purely for enjoyment, do not get paid and usually have a full-time job.

- **Professionals** take part in a sport, or an activity, as their livelihood. They get paid for taking part and it is their full-time job.

There are also two other types of sportspeople who should be considered:

- **Shamateurs** are people who claim to be amateurs but are actually paid to take part. Payments they receive would be illegal and unofficial under the rules of the sport in which they take part.

- **Semi-professionals** have a job but also take part in sport, for which they are legitimately paid. Some have full-time jobs and only take part in their sport in their spare time and others have paid part-time jobs and spend the rest of their time at their sport.

Not all people who take part in sport fit neatly into any of these categories and it is often very difficult, in certain sports, to tell which is which. It is quite unusual to find anyone competing at the highest level in any sport who is truly an amateur because of the demands for training, practising, travelling and performing which would prevent them having a full-time job as well.

In **open sports**, such as golf, it is possible for amateurs and professionals to compete together. If there is prize money to be won, the amateurs are not usually allowed to keep it, so there may be a special award for the best-placed amateur in the competition.

Historical background

Before about 1900 there were very few sports with professional players, although it was quite common for wealthy people to play sport full-time. There simply was not enough money generated by sport at that time to pay people to play.

Cricket was one of the few sports with players who had the time, and independent means of income, to play. These players generally did not need to work for a living, so they were able to dedicate themselves to their chosen sport. They were called **true amateurs** because they received no payments or rewards for taking part, other than perhaps a trophy if they won.

Cricket's influence

In cricket there were:

- the **gentlemen**, who were wealthy and played for fun

- the **players**, who were paid to play, although it was usually only a comparatively small amount.

Most county cricket clubs could only afford one or two 'players', who were the paid professionals for the club. The rest of the team would be made up of wealthy 'gentlemen' and other amateurs.

Many sports have only become properly organized within the last hundred years or so. This has clearly had an effect on the overall growth of professional sport. The first cricket **test match** did not take place until 1877, which was the same year that the first Wimbledon tennis championship tournament was played.

The governing body of athletics is the Amateur Athletic Association, known as the three 'A's. It was not formed until 1880 and the first soccer **World Cup** was not played until 1930. This has meant that many sports do not have the same tradition of professional players that cricket does.

Many sports first had to be properly organized, stadiums built for spectators, sponsorship obtained and media interest generated before there was enough income and money to support professionals. Even now, many sports do not have professional players at any level because the sport does not generate enough money to pay them.

All sports started as amateur, but the majority now have professionals who take part at the highest levels, as well as amateurs who play at lower levels. Most sports have their own rules about what is allowed, for a player to maintain his or her **amateur status**.

A very early cricket match featuring 'gentlemen' and 'players'

Changes towards open sport

There were professional players in tennis as long ago as 1926 but these players were not allowed to play in any of the major world events (known as the **Grand Slam** events). They had to play in specially arranged tournaments. This situation existed until 1968 when Wimbledon finally broke down the barriers between the amateurs and professionals and ran the first open tournament. This influenced the organizers of many other sports, who could see that the barriers needed to be removed officially. Players in most of the sports had managed to find ways around the rules anyway – these will be considered later!

Rod Laver, the winner of the first open Wimbledon in 1968

In 1988 tennis was re-admitted to the Olympic Games. It was one of several sports that were allowed into the Olympic programme despite previously being considered as professional sports. In fact, the Olympic movement changed their rules to allow amateurs to receive prize money and appearance money. Professional sportspeople such as tennis players and basketball players now compete openly in the Olympics. The number of sports included in the Olympic programme increases with each Games, and more of the traditionally professional games are being admitted. When the 'Dream Team' American basketball squad (the whole squad was made up of full-time professional basketball players) was allowed to compete at the 1992 Barcelona Games, there was a great deal of controversy and media criticism. Since then this state of affairs has been accepted more.

Another sport which had maintained very strict barriers between amateurs and professionals was rugby football. There were two forms of rugby created in 1895, when there was a dispute over professional and amateur status. Then, in 1995, the sport took on open status. The players were allowed to play both versions if they wished, and they could be paid for playing either. Up until then there had been no professional rugby union players allowed at all.

The growth and development of professional rugby has meant that players are now able to play all the year round. The standards of the game have improved as the players are able to train full-time as well! Many players now play rugby league for part of the season and rugby union for the rest. The rugby league organizers have made their sport a summer activity instead of a winter one.

Overcoming the rules

There were, and still are, many ways of getting around the rules which amateur sportspeople were supposed to obey. These include:

- *Trust funds* – money earned through sport is paid into a fund which is not supposed to be used while the sportsperson is actually performing, but is only to be used when they 'retire'. This was a very popular method among rugby players and athletes.

- *Occupations* – some of the 'jobs' which sportspeople have are specifically arranged to allow them to take part in their sport and get a wage. They are just token occupations with responsibilities which do not actually involve them in doing any proper work at all. In many countries being a member of any of the uniformed services is just such a career. Many of the former communist countries of Europe had entire teams drawn from their armies.

- *Scholarships* – many universities and colleges offer sports scholarships which allow almost full-time sport to be played, with little or no actual studying required.

- *Expenses payments* – these are often far higher than actually needed, and effectively amount to payment for taking part.

- *Illegal payments* – this is often referred to as **boot money**, from the practice of putting money in players' boots at the end of a match as a way of paying them, illegally, for performing.

A professional rugby league player in action

- *Gifts* – items such as luxury cars are given as prizes or gifts, then these can be traded in for cash.

- *Sponsorship* – all the various ways this can be administered can be used to the advantage of the performers.

4 Drugs and sport

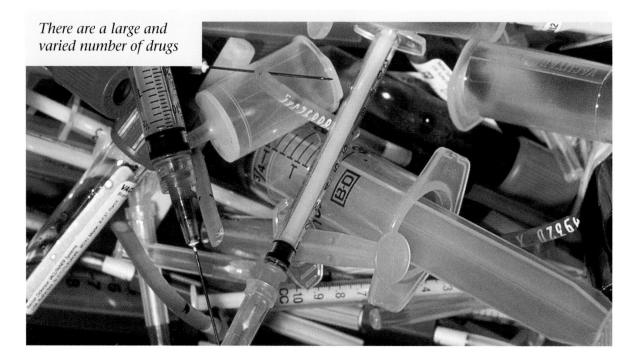

There are a large and varied number of drugs

The whole issue of drug-taking by sportspeople is very controversial, and has been especially so over recent years.

Drug-taking in sport has gone on for many years but it has increased in recent times, due to:

- the highly advanced types of drugs which are now available;

- the pressures and high financial rewards, which can tempt a performer to use them.

What are drugs?

A drug is a chemical substance which, when introduced into the body, can alter the biochemical system.

Most drugs are designed to improve an imbalance caused by a disease or an illness. For example, a simple and common drug is paracetamol. If you take paracetamol for a headache, the pain goes away because of the changes caused in your body. However, when drugs are used in a healthy body they do not always have the desired effect. All drugs have some sort of **side effects**.

The law and drugs

In 1971 the Misuse of Drugs Act was introduced in the UK. It identified a list of dangerous or harmful substances and called them **controlled drugs**. These fall into three categories, or classes, and there are different penalties for unauthorized possession or abuse of these substances. These classes are based on the potential harmfulness of each drug. The main ones listed are:

- *Class A* – opium, heroin, methadone, morphine, hallucinogens (such as LSD), injectable amphetamines and 'designer drugs' such as 'ecstasy';

- *Class B* – opiate drugs, certain barbiturates, cannabis resin, and six stimulant drugs of the amphetamine group

- *Class C* – other amphetamine drugs, 36 benzodiazepine tranquillizers and several non-barbiturate sedatives.

These drugs are often called **social drugs** because they are used by all sorts of people in society for a variety of reasons, but they are, nevertheless, illegal.

The penalties for conviction range from life imprisonment for a Class A drug to two years imprisonment and/or an unlimited fine for a Class C drug.

There is evidence of sportspeople using these drugs (some examples will be considered later), but there is little to indicate that their performance is improved. In many cases using these drugs would be a disadvantage. However, if a player is found to be using any of the drugs listed above they would probably face a police prosecution. In addition, the governing body of their sport would discipline them.

Most sportspeople who are involved in drug-taking do so in the hope that it will make them perform better. These drugs are known as **performance-enhancing drugs**. They are banned by the International Olympic Committee (**IOC**) and are therefore banned throughout the world. In 1993 the IOC identified the following classes of drugs which it refers to as **doping classes**:

- A – stimulants

- B – narcotic analgesics

- C – anabolic agents

- D – diuretics

- E – peptide and glycoprotein hormones and analogues.

In addition to the drugs listed above, the Committee also identified these classes which were subject to certain restrictions:

- A – alcohol

- B – marijuana

- C – local anaesthetics

- D – corticosteroids

- E – beta blockers.

Apart from marijuana, these drugs are not strictly illegal, although it is illegal to deal in, sell, supply or obtain anabolic steroids. The governing bodies of sport have banned their use and taken steps to stop performers from using them.

It is the fact that using these drugs can actually improve a player's performance that has led to their being banned. This may seem confusing when some of them, such as alcohol and local anaesthetics, are so easily available. These substances can be used to advantage but, more importantly, they can have damaging side effects.

Doping classes

The IOC has made its position clear on doping: 'Doping contravenes the ethics of both sports and medical science' it has said. The IOC medical commission bans:

- the administration of substances belonging to the selected classes of pharmacological agents: stimulants, narcotics, anabolic agents, diuretics, peptide hormones and analogues

- the use of various doping methods: **blood doping**, pharmacological, chemical and physical manipulations.

The second category covers very general areas because the battle against drug use is a constant one and new drugs and cheating methods are constantly being discovered and outlawed.

The types and effects of these banned groups are detailed below.

Stimulants

These substances increase alertness, reduce fatigue (extreme physical tiredness in the body or muscles which can prevent a performer carrying on) and may increase a user's competitiveness and hostility. They can also produce a loss of judgement and this can obviously be potentially dangerous and lead to accidents in some sports. An overdose of stimulants can even cause death. This has happened twice in cycling events – once in an Olympic event and once in the Tour de France event. Other side effects can include:

- high blood pressure and headaches;

- strokes and increased and irregular heartbeats;

- anxiety and tremors;

- insensitivity to serious injuries;

- addiction.

There is an unusual group of stimulant drugs known as **beta2agonists** that are classed as being both stimulants and anabolic agents.

Many of the compounds found in stimulants are also found in the treatments for colds, hay fever and asthma, so it is very important to check with a pharmacist before you take any medications before an event. Top performers always have to keep a very detailed record of any medications they are taking, so that they can disclose them during any drug-testing procedure and they can be taken into consideration later. The testing procedure is very thorough and will show up traces of any drugs which the performer has taken, even if they have taken them with good reason.

Another recognized stimulant is caffeine, which is normally found in both tea and coffee! There is a maximum level of 12 micrograms per millilitre, above which it would be considered to be performance-enhancing. Cocaine is another stimulant and it is one of the controlled and therefore illegal drugs.

It is fairly easy to identify sporting activities where the use of stimulants could possibly improve performance. Unfortunately, many performers have taken them in the past to help them keep going whilst competing or to work harder when they are training.

Narcotic analgesics

These include morphine, heroin and codeine. The main reason they are banned is because they hide the effects of illness and injury. Codeine for instance is found in many pain killers, some of which are freely available and can be taken in tablet form for headaches and 'flu symptoms. They suppress the feeling of pain but their side effects are:

- respiratory depression

- physical and psychological dependence

- exhaustion or over training

- constipation

- extreme apathy (lack of interest in what you are doing).

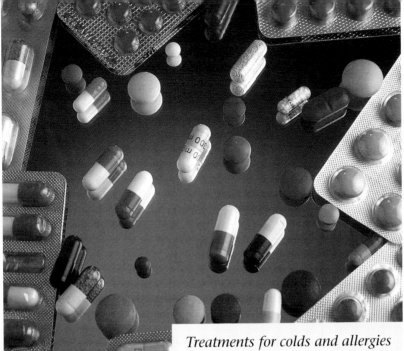

Treatments for colds and allergies may contain banned substances

- **androgenic** – this promotes the development of male characteristics

- **anabolic** – stimulates the build-up of muscle tissue.

More than a hundred types of anabolic steroids are available. The most common ones are **nandrolone**, **testosterone**, **stanozolol**, and **boldenone**. They are usually taken in tablet form, but some of the steroids are taken by injection directly into the muscles.

Steroids were developed originally because they helped to cure anaemic conditions (a lack of iron in the body), eased wasting conditions and bone diseases and were useful in the treatment of breast cancer. They are used quite extensively by hospitals in the treatment of many conditions and can even be life-saving.

Unfortunately, sports performers began to see some of the possible benefits from taking this type of drug. The first recorded cases of performers taking them were in the 1950s when some body-builders and weight-lifters started to use them.

This has now spread to many other sports where the performers feel that it can help their performance by:

- increasing muscle strength

- enabling them to train harder and for longer

- increasing their competitiveness.

Performers must be very careful to draw the line between treating an injury and actually concealing its full extent by taking narcotic analgesics. A far more serious injury might occur if the drugs are hiding the effects of something that started off as relatively minor. The body normally needs time to recover, and taking these drugs can mean that this process does not occur. The drugs will not cure the problem but will only be a temporary way of overcoming the symptoms. Obviously, with the pressures of many competitions, performers may inevitably be tempted!

Anabolic agents

These are probably the best known and most commonly abused drugs in sport. They are certainly the ones which have been the most controversial and most discussed in the media. The main type is **androgenic anabolic steroids** (most commonly called **steroids**). These are both natural and synthetic compounds which are very similar to the natural male hormone, testosterone. Testosterone has two main effects:

There is no real evidence to back up claims that these drugs can have such a marked effect, but there is evidence to suggest that they can help with training. Taking steroids can enable a performer to work harder in training sessions. Because of this they are often called **training drugs**. They are often used during the build-up to a season or a competition or tournament. The performer stops taking the drug far enough in advance of the competition to make sure that no traces of it are found during pre-event testing. This can make it very difficult to detect the use of the drug, and it is the reason why many of the sports governing bodies reserve the right to drug-test their performers at any time during the year, and often during their training periods.

A sprinter who uses steroids as a training aid would only need a ten per cent improvement to change from being a borderline international athlete to become a world record holder. This fact has led to several performers giving in to the temptation.

Risks

The risks involved in taking steroids are quite serious, and the list of side effects is horrific.

- **Liver disorders and heart disease** – there can be serious damage to the liver structure, leading to jaundice, liver failure, liver tumours and bleeding in the liver. In one case a 26-year-old body-builder who had been using steroids for several years died of cancer of the liver as direct result of taking the drugs. The heart can be affected by changes in its fatty substance.

The margin between winning and losing can be a very small one

This can lead to an increased liability to heart attacks and strokes, as well as increased blood pressure.

- **Sexual and physique problems** – in children, growth can be affected or even stunted. Remember that in some sports such as gymnastics, performers start serious training while they are still children. They could be tempted to use drugs, or even encouraged to do so by adults who should know better. Men can suffer from reduced sperm production and even sterility, preventing them from fathering children. There can be shrinking of the testicles, impotence and even the growth of breasts in men. Women can have a disruption of the menstrual cycle and ovulation, changes in the sex organs, balding, acne, growth of facial hair and deepening of the voice. Steroids can cause miscarriage, still-birth or damage to the foetus, especially during early pregnancy.

- **Behavioural effects** – there can be quite marked changes in behaviour in some individuals. There may be increased moodiness, mood swings and aggression. The changes can be so extreme that they actually constitute a psychiatric disorder, then the person affected needs specialist medical help. There are several recorded instances of the wives of body-builders who have been taking steroids reporting that they have become very aggressive and violent as a result.

How much a user is affected by these side effects and disorders depends upon the type and amount of steroids being taken and the period of time over which they are used. The effects can be reversed if their use is stopped soon enough. Remember also that the beta2agonists are also classed as stimulants. They have anabolic effects, and can have similar side effects too.

The side effects of corticosteroids are also quite serious. They include:

- high blood pressure;

- salt and water retention;

- potassium loss;

- bone and muscle weakness;

- mental disturbances such as euphoria (an extreme feeling of well being or optimism), depression or paranoia (an extreme feeling of being persecuted or picked on);

- diabetes;

- suppression of growth in children.

All of these side effects have been shown to exist, so it is not surprising that the authorities ban the use of these drugs actually to protect the performers. What is amazing is that any of the performers continue to use them, knowing just how damaging they can be.

Diuretics

Used under medical supervision, these drugs reduce excess body fluids and help control high blood pressure. Sports performers could misuse them like this:

- to reduce weight quickly in sports where weight categories are important (Activities such as boxing or any of the martial arts have particular, very strict weight categories which the competitors must fit into. Also, in some sports such as gymnastics, it is an advantage to be lightweight.)

- to reduce the concentration of substances by diluting the urine.

Because of this second effect, some authorities reserve the right to obtain urine samples from competitors at the weigh-in prior to a competition. A weight loss achieved artificially, by means of these drugs, could be dangerous for the performer as it weakens the body. There are recorded examples of jockeys taking these drugs.

Use of beta blockers is banned in shooting events

Peptide and glycoprotein hormones and analogues

These drugs are based on substances which occur naturally in the body and are therefore quite difficult to detect when used illegally. Possibly for this reason, they are being used increasingly by performers. They fall into four main categories as follows:

- *Chorionic gonadotrophin* (HCC – Human Chorionic Gonadotrophin) has the effect of increasing the existing levels of androgenic steroids in the body and also increases levels of the male hormone testosterone.

- *Corticotrophin* (ACTH) is used to increase the levels of corticosteroids and increase the levels of euphoria which they give.

- *Growth hormone* (HGH, somatrophin) is used to increase growth and can have some very serious side effects. A disease called Creutzfeldt Jacob's disease, which affects the nervous system, can be contracted when growth hormone is obtained from impure sources. This can prove fatal.

- **Erythropoietin** (EPO) occurs naturally in the kidneys and regulates the production of red blood cells. It can have a similar effect to blood doping, which will be considered later.

All of the above banned substances are already present in the human body but drug misuse increases the levels artificially. If these higher levels are detected, the sportsperson can be banned.

Beta-blockers

These are drugs that are prescribed to people who have a medical condition affecting their heart. They calm and control the heart rate. In some activities, they would not be of any real benefit, but in others they have been identified as advantageous, since they can have a calming effect, for example stopping any minor shakes when the player is shooting or concentrating. Beta-blockers are therefore banned in:

- archery

- shooting

- modern pentathlon (shooting events are included here)

- diving and synchronized swimming

- bobsleigh

- luge (a form of bobsleigh)

- ski jumping

- free-style skiing

- snooker.

The use of beta-blockers in events requiring endurance would actually harm the player's performance, but there have been cases where they have been used in sports to calm nerves and keep the performer steady.

Fact File

Canadian snooker player Bill Werbenek was banned from playing snooker because he was taking beta-blockers. He had been officially prescribed them for a heart condition but was not allowed to carry on playing whilst still taking them.

Blood doping

Some years ago, endurance athletes used this technique to make their blood more efficient in carrying and supplying oxygen. In blood doping, extra blood is added into the bloodstream. This blood may have been taken from the same athlete previously, forcing the remaining blood to produce extra red blood cells to replace those lost. When the blood is added back into the bloodstream, there is an increased number of red blood cells which can carry extra oxygen around the body. As oxygen is one of the main sources of energy used over an extended period of time by any athlete taking part in long distance endurance events, this was clearly giving them an unfair advantage. Although it is more common to use the athlete's own blood, it can also be done with someone else's blood, red blood cells or related products.

This used to be tolerated, and some athletes openly admitted that it was something which they did, but it is now banned. Possible side effects include:

- development of allergic reactions such as a rash or fever

- acute kidney damage if the incorrect blood type is used

- delayed transfusion reaction which can result in a fever and jaundice

- transmission of infectious diseases such as viruses, hepatitis and AIDS

- overload of the circulation and metabolic shock.

As well as banning blood doping, the IOC has also banned any interference by what it calls pharmacological, chemical and physical manipulation. This covers such things as interfering with urine samples or using medical knowledge to assist performers.

Doping control

The use of drugs to improve performance is clearly cheating. It can also be harmful, sometimes even fatal. Some performers use a variety of drugs from the different categories in an attempt to improve their performance, despite all the warnings and evidence of the harm it is doing them.

Their use is banned and there are procedures in force to try to catch those who do use drugs, and to discourage others from doing so. The procedure is called **doping control** and it involves obtaining a urine sample, testing it for any banned substances and following that up with any disciplinary procedures which might be necessary.

How doping control works

The testing procedure is as follows and it is the step-by-step process which all performers must go through if they are tested for drugs:

I. Notifying the athlete

Competitors can be notified in writing that they have been selected for test. They will be allowed to finish their training before they report to the Doping Control Station at a stated time. In many competitions they will be asked to report immediately after the sporting event has taken place.

2. Reporting for testing

They may be accompanied to the Doping Control Station where sealed, non-alcoholic, drinks are available and a representative from the sports governing body might be present.

3. Selecting a collection vessel

They choose the container for the urine sample from the selection available. These containers are all numbered.

4. Providing a sample under supervision

The competitor removes enough clothing to satisfy the Independent Sampling Officer (**ISO**), who must be able to observe the sample being given. Only the competitor handles the sample and returns to the administration room.

5. Selecting the sample containers

The competitor is allowed to select two containers between which the urine sample will be divided.

6. Breaking the security seals

The competitor breaks the security seals on the bottles or containers.

7. Dividing the sample

The sample is divided between the A and B sample bottles.

8. Sealing the samples

The ISO checks the bottle top seals and then the competitor actually seals up the containers, labelling them A and B.

9. Recording the information

The bottle code numbers and seal numbers are filled in and checked by the competitor, who may then declare any medications which they have taken the previous week.

10. Certifying the information

The ISO, the competitor and the competitor's representative (if present) then sign a form if they are satisfied with the procedure. A copy of the Doping Control Collection Form is given to the competitor who is then free to go.

I I. Transferring the samples to the laboratory

Both the samples are sent by a secure system to an accredited laboratory for analysis. Only the sample, seal and medication information is forwarded. The competitor's name, or any other information is not included.

12. Reporting the result

The report is usually available within ten days. If the result is negative, the governing body is informed and the B sample is destroyed. Results can be given within 24 hours if a major competition is under way. This is certainly the case in the Olympics where the first three athletes in all events are routinely tested.

If the result is positive the following procedure starts:

- The competitor may be suspended from competition and the second sample can be analysed. The competitor is also allowed to present their case.

- A decision is made on the punishment to be given. This can range from suspension for a given period of time, to a lifetime ban.

- Every competitor is allowed to appeal against the decisions.

The above procedure is thought to be as fair as possible. If a competitor refuses to be tested, it is considered to be the same as providing a positive sample and punishments will be set.

Recommended sanctions

The following sanctions can be imposed following a positive test:

- *Scale 1* (all the main listed doping classes) – two-year ban for the first offence, life ban for the second offence

- *Scale 2* (ephedrine, phenylpropanolamine etc.) – a maximum three-month ban for the first offence, two years for the second offence and a life ban for the third offence.

Drug abuse in sport

Unfortunately, the sanctions described for use of illegal drugs in sport have been imposed. The first recorded use of drugs dates from 1865. There are many other recorded cases where performers have used drugs to improve their performance. Some of the most notorious landmarks in drug testing are listed below:

- *1955* – 25 urine test were carried out on cyclists in a race in France and five proved positive.

- *1962* – The IOC passed a resolution against doping.

- *1965* – The Sports Council formed a working party on drug abuse in sport.

- *1967* – The cyclist, Tommy Simpson, collapsed and died during the Tour de France race due to an overdose of amphetamine.

- *1968* – Drug testing was introduced to the Winter and Summer Olympics. Interestingly, not one sample proved positive, which started a debate over whether the sport was clean, or that the testing was outdated and inadequate and was simply not catching the guilty people. In the same year the Belgian marathon runner, Joseph Ronbaux was banned for life for taking drugs.

- *1970* – Drug tests were first introduced to the Commonwealth Games.

- *1976* – The first tests for steroids were introduced.

- *1988* – In the Seoul Olympics there were ten positive doping results.

Ben Johnson, who has twice been banned for drug use

Five of these were in the weight-lifting, two in the modern pentathlon, one each in wrestling and judo and one in athletics. The athlete found guilty was Ben Johnson. This was one of the most famous cases of drug abuse as he had just won the Olympic 100-metres championship. Johnson was given a two-year ban, after which he returned to racing with little success. He then subsequently failed another test and was banned from the sport altogether.

- *1992* – Three British competitors at the Barcelona Olympics were sent home in disgrace after testing positive and failing the drug test. They were sprinter Jason Livingstone and weight-lifters Andrew Saxon and Andrew Davies. There were several other positive tests on other nations' athletes.

There is little in sport more controversial than the drug situation and several athletes have battled against the authorities after their bans.

- *1989* – Trine Hattestad, the women's European javelin champion, was given a two-year ban for taking steroids. The ban was set aside and she was awarded $50,000 compensation when it was decided that the amount found was too small to be significant.

- *1990* – The American world 400-metre champion, Butch Reynolds was found guilty of taking steroids and claimed mistaken identity. He took his appeal all the way to the US Supreme Court but still had to serve a two-year suspension. He returned to competition after the ban and continued to protest his innocence but had probably missed out on his potentially most successful period as an athlete due to the ban.

- *1991* – The German world 100-metre and 200-metre champion Katrin Krabbe successfully appealed against manipulation of a test in 1991 on a legal technicality. She also escaped on a technicality in 1992 after traces of the beta2agonist clenbuturol were found but was eventually banned for bringing the sport into disrepute.

- *1994* – Diane Modahl, a British middle distance runner, was tested positive for traces of testosterone. She appealed against the test which had shown her to have 42 times the normal amount. There was great controversy about how her sample had been stored at the laboratory to which it had been sent. The abnormally high amounts found suggested that there had been some mistake. The first appeal failed and it was not until 1995 that she was eventually cleared. As with Butch Reynolds before her, she returned to athletics but was unable to achieve her previous best due to the time she had been forced out of competition.

China

China as a nation had not taken part in international competition for many years but when they returned with competitors in the early 1990s there was much suspicion about the standards they managed to achieve. Their runners and swimmers, in particular, dominated in many events despite not having competed outside their own country previously. After many complaints from other countries the Chinese began to drug-test their performers.

Following the World Swimming Championships in 1994, seven Chinese swimmers tested positive for drug use. All had been using a form of the male hormone testosterone, which acted as a steroid. This brief period of sporting dominance stopped almost as soon as the regular drug testing was started and the suspicions of other countries seemed to be justified.

Two cases

Two other drug-related cases in 1994 showed the differing attitudes of the authorities themselves both to drug-taking by sportspeople, and to the types of drugs being used.

Within days of each other, in December 1994 both Paul Merson (Arsenal and England soccer player) and Jamie Bloem (Doncaster and South African rugby league player) were involved in drug scandals. Merson admitted being addicted to cocaine and alcohol, and Bloem tested positive for anabolic steroids.

The governing bodies of each sport acted and Merson was sent to a drug rehabilitation centre for six weeks and ordered to be monitored and treated for eighteen months after that. In fact, Merson returned to first team football within two months, and in 1997 he was recalled to the full England national squad. The impression given was that because he had taken 'social drugs' (rather than performance-enhancing ones) he needed help and treatment rather than punishment.

Bloem, on the other hand was banned for two years, and his governing body considered whether to increase future bans to four years. They had a particular set penalty which was enforced for any use of performance-enhancing drugs. This penalty was imposed with no consideration given to helping the performer with any identified drug problem.

5 Politics and sport

Politicians have helped increase safety and control at stadiums

It is almost impossible to keep politics out of sport. Sport in most countries is financed, or at least monitored, from government level and is therefore inter-related with politics.

The UK has a minister responsible for sport who is very influential and can advise the various sporting bodies. In some countries, especially the former communist countries, sport was a political priority area. The state was in complete control of it.

The degree of control in the old communist countries was shown when they boycotted some of the Olympic Games (for example, in 1980) and refused to send their athletes. Their political systems meant that they could do this. In a similar situation the UK could only advise their athletes against going and could not actually stop them from taking part.

Politics assisting sport

It is often thought that politicians only influence sport in a negative way, but this is not strictly true. In the UK, without government backing there would be far less provision of facilities and funding. Past and present governments have also ensured that sport is, by law, part of the range of educational subjects which must be taught in schools, within a varied PE programme.

Another positive move has been the setting up of various sports bodies such as the Sports Council, and the provision of extra funds from such sources as the National Lottery.

If there are any major problems associated with sport then the Government will act.

The Taylor enquiry which followed the Heysall Stadium disaster and the Hillsborough disaster was set up to find solutions to the problems of controlling large crowds in stadiums and making adequate provision for them. The results of this enquiry were welcomed and money was made available to help with the improvements which benefited all types of sports.

There is no doubt that in many communist countries the political systems raised the standards of sport. Sport was given a very high profile. The athletes and sportspeople in those countries would not have considered that their government was interfering with sport, but were more likely to think it was giving valuable assistance.

The collapse of the former communist countries in 1990 was a major turning point in the way in which sport was organized there. The growth of democratic governments meant that the old ways of running sport – under tight government control – changed drastically. However, the loss of the large amounts of money that had previously been spent on sport led to a decrease in standards in many of these countries.

Political Issues

The relationship between politics and sport has not always been easy, and has often been very controversial. There have been many occasions when politics have interfered with sport. Some are listed here.

The Berlin wall was pulled down in 1992

- *1908* – The Finnish team at the Olympics was forced to parade without its flag because Russia, who ruled Finland at that time, refused to authorize it. The American team did not like decisions made by the all-British appeal jury and staged a demonstration in New York.

- *1912* – There were more protests by Russia that Finland should not have its own flag, and the Austro-Hungarian Empire protested that Bohemia and Hungary should not be allowed to compete separately.

There was also a very strong rumour, which was never proved, that the black American sprinter, Howard Drew, was withdrawn from the 100-metres final so that the winner would not be a black athlete. The official reason given for his withdrawal was that he had injured a tendon. The Swedish newspapers claimed that he was locked in the changing rooms by his own officials during the final!

- *1920* – The Olympic Games were held in Antwerp, Belgium immediately after World War I. Germany, and its wartime allies, were not sent an invitation to take part.

- *1925* – The year following the Paris Olympics, the Soviet Union Communist Party made a declaration that 'sport should be used as a means of rallying the broad masses of workers and peasants around the various Party and trade union organizations through which the masses of workers and peasants are to be drawn into social and political activity'. This set the tone for the communist attitude towards sport for the next 65 years and made it an obvious political tool.

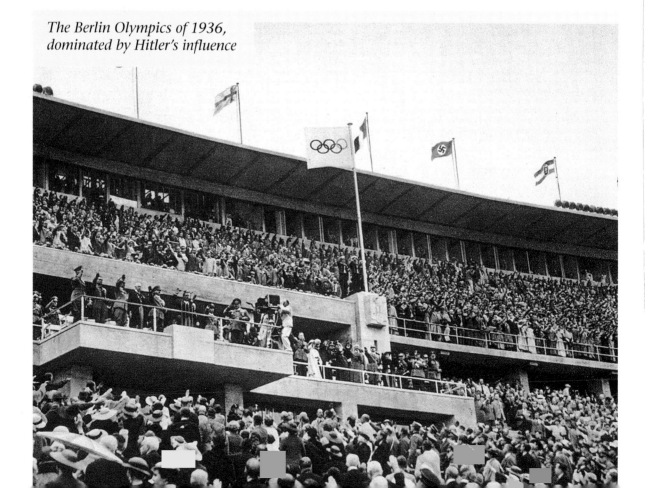

The Berlin Olympics of 1936, dominated by Hitler's influence

- *1936* – The Olympics were held in Berlin, Germany. In 1933, Adolph Hitler had come to power and the country was ruled by the Nazi party. Hitler decided to use the games as a massive **propaganda exercise** (a way of sending out misleading and biased information). He believed that there was a master race in Germany known as the Aryans and that Jews and other races and religions were to be despised and persecuted. He had already started to persecute the Jews in Germany and many of the other countries' teams considered boycotting the Games. The decision to hold the Games in Berlin had been made in 1931, when the political situation had not been foreseen.

The Games were really dominated by one man, Jesse Owens, the black American athlete, who won four gold medals. His success, along with that of the rest of the black Americans in the US team, was a great embarrassment to Hitler and ensured that his plans to prove the supremacy of Aryons failed.

- *1940–4* – There were no Olympic Games held, and very few other sporting contests either, as most major countries were fighting World War II. Although some sport carried on at a local level in some countries, it was impossible to have properly organized international sport.

- *1948* – South Africa introduced the **apartheid** laws which enforced a policy of racial segregation within that country. This meant that black and non-white people were denied rights, as well as facilities and opportunities. They were not considered for any of the national teams in any sporting areas and had to lead separate lives from the white population. This led to a great deal of criticism from other countries throughout the world. It became a major political issue, causing many problems in South Africa's relationships with other countries for years afterwards.

- *1949* – A New Zealand rugby team was banned from touring South Africa because the team contained Maori players, who would not be considered acceptable under the apartheid laws introduced there.

- *1954* – China was finally admitted to the Olympics, despite not accepting the **IOC** decision to recognize its neighbour state of Taiwan which China still refused to acknowledge.

- *1954* – China withdrew from the Olympic movement (over the dispute about Taiwan) and started a boycott of sports organizations and competitions.

- *1964* – South Africa was banned from the Olympic movement because of the apartheid laws. This led to a long period of demonstrations and boycotts throughout the world. The South Africans even arranged **rebel tours** where they paid foreign sport stars to come and play against them (mainly rugby and cricket players). The performers who took part were often subsequently banned in their own countries as a result.

- *1970* – A state of war was declared between Honduras and El Salvador after a **World Cup** qualifying game. Also the South African cricket team was asked not to tour England after a formal request from the British Home Secretary, James Callaghan.

- *1976* – Some African countries boycotted the Montreal Olympics as a protest against New Zealand having sent a rugby team to South Africa.

- *1980* – The USA and 51 other nations boycotted the Moscow Olympics as a protest against the Soviet Union's invasion of their neighbouring country, Afghanistan.

- *1984* – The Soviet Union and fourteen other nations boycotted the Los Angeles Olympics, mainly as retaliation for the action taken in 1980, but officially for security reasons and as a protest over the commercialization of the Games.

- *1990* – The communist states in Eastern Europe began to crumble after political change. Many smaller nations were formed, which joined in world sport.

- *1992* – South Africa finally abolished the apartheid system and was re-admitted to world sport and the Barcelona Olympic games where they fielded a mixed team.

The readmitted South African team in 1992, Barcelona

6 Technological change and sport

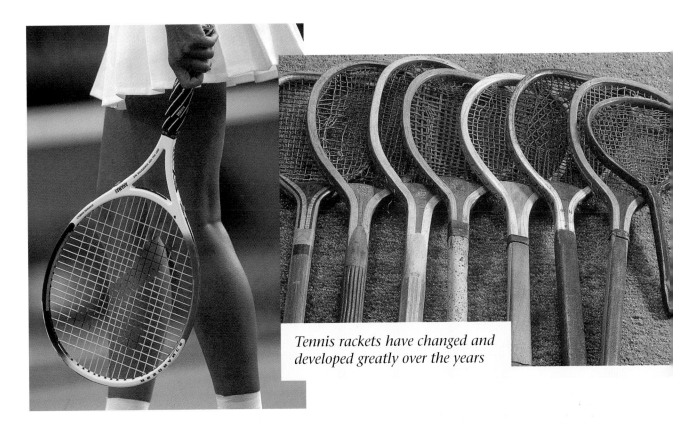

Tennis rackets have changed and developed greatly over the years

Throughout the history of sport there has been continual – if gradual – change and improvement. However, the developments have been far more rapid in recent years. The major changes have been in equipment and materials.

Equipment

Equipment for players

The equipment available nowadays for people taking part in sport is far more varied, safer, and better designed than it has ever been before. It is also constantly changing – so much so that governing bodies have to keep checks to ensure that it is legal and does not give anyone an unfair advantage. The impact these changes have made can be seen in these particular sports:

● *Racket sports* – it is only over the last twenty years or so that wooden rackets have been replaced by ones made of aluminium, then graphite. Using these new, lighter materials has enabled the head, and therefore the ball-striking area, to be enlarged, without changing the overall length of the racket. Rackets for tennis, squash and badminton are all made from these newer materials.

There is no longer any need for racket presses, which protected the rackets and stopped them from warping, as the new materials are lighter, stronger and more stable. It is not only the rackets themselves which have new materials. Synthetic materials are also used to string the rackets, and these can give extra power to the performers.

Fact File

The javelin has undergone many changes as more advanced materials have been used in its construction. However, they became so efficient that they became dangerous. Competitors were throwing them so far that the stadiums were not big enough. Therefore they are now reduced in weight and the position of the centre of gravity has been moved, to reduce the distances they can be thrown. This was an example of technology being too effective!

Most sporting footwear is now very specialized and specific to the sport

- *Athletics* – field events have benefited from improved equipment in several ways. In the modern pole vault, the pole is constructed from a lightweight fibreglass compound which makes it lighter, stronger and more flexible than the older versions. This means that the vaulters can jump much higher. For increased safety, large air-filled and purpose-built landing areas have been designed which are more suitable and efficient for use with modern equipment. They can allow a jumper to land safely after coming down from a height of nearly seven metres (about 20 feet). Previously the jumpers would have landed in a sand pit! The high jump also has a similar landing area which enables the jumpers to use the technique of the **Fosbury Flop** (named after the first person to perform it – Dick Fosbury), without fear of harming themselves when they land on their backs.

Footwear has also undergone significant change and in athletics, specialist shoes are now available for any of the events. With the changes and advances in the running surfaces, this is quite essential for an athlete. Where winning margins are so close, they must make sure that they have the most modern equipment available.

- *Cricket* – there is now a full range of protective equipment available for cricket players. Although the basic leg guard pads have not changed significantly there is now a full range of protective equipment for the head and the materials used for the other protective items are lighter and less bulky than they were. This means that the player is protected but does not lose any mobility.

Equipment for administration

As well as changes in equipment for the performer there have also been advances in technology which can help to make the sport fair, and life easier for those who are officiating. They include:

- *Accurate timing* – in events where it is essential that the timing is completely accurate, the possibility of human error has been reduced by the introduction of sophisticated machines. Electronic sensors in sprinters' starting blocks start the timing as soon as the performers leave the blocks. They are so sensitive that they can even detect a false start. They are linked to the starting gun and can register the athlete's reaction time. Other sensors register the runners as they cross the line and there is an instant readout of the measured time, which can be displayed on TV monitor screens. A championship can be decided by one-thousandth of a second and it is only these very accurate timing devices which can separate some of the runners.

  In tennis, similar devices are used to check whether the ball is in or out of play, especially on the lines, as the ball is often travelling too fast for the human eye to judge accurately.

- *Accurate officiating* – many sports are using the advanced technology of television to help the officials. One of the first sports to do this was American Football. At every game, there is a booth where extra officials check replayed action, to decide whether or not the officials in the game have made correct decisions. This spread to cricket where the **third umpire** is now very common in international games. The umpires on the pitch can ask for a decision to be made for them after the extra umpire watches the TV action replayed. This technique is also used in soccer. The first TV-assisted match was played in Paris in April 1997. There were 24 cameras to watch the play, and headphones and microphones were used to allow the referee and fourth official to keep in contact. Electronic wrist-bands worn by the players tracked them for offside decisions, and microchips in the ball even showed whether it was in or out of play!

Cycling competitor at the Atlanta Olympics, wears a heart-rate monitor

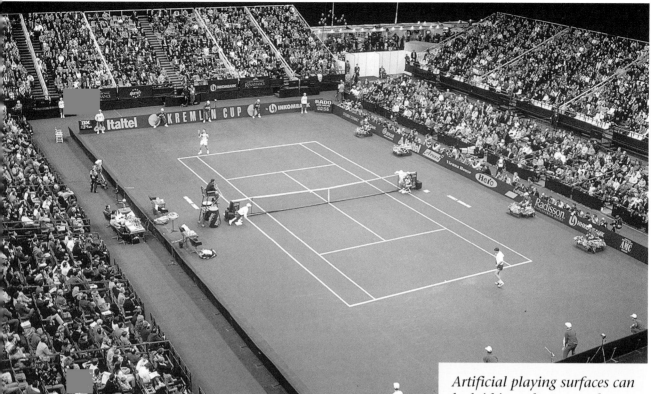

Artificial playing surfaces can be laid just about anywhere

- **Monitoring performances** – players can be helped to monitor their own performance as it is underway. It is now very common for cyclists taking part in long-distance events to have chest harnesses which constantly monitor their heart rates. These are linked up to monitors either on the handlebars or their wrists. The system enables them to work at their highest capacity and can also warn them if they are working at too high a level.

Materials

The choice of synthetic materials now available for use in sport is very wide. They range from the light, aerodynamic materials used for clothing for swimmers, speed skaters and cyclists, right through to the variety of artificial surfaces used for

tennis, hockey, soccer, athletics and in sports halls. Previously it was only possible to use natural materials such as wood, metal, cotton, wool and leather for clothing and equipment.

The development of improved materials for playing surfaces has greatly changed the nature of some of the games. Top-class hockey is now played almost exclusively on artificial surfaces and very rarely on grass. This allows the players to benefit far more from high levels of skill, as the ball does not move about as much as it would on a bumpy grass pitch.

Artificial strips for cricket are becoming more and more popular and artificial surfaces for tennis can now be laid down almost anywhere, to enable tennis tournaments and matches to be played.

Not all sports have totally endorsed these new surfaces. Both soccer and American Football authorities initially allowed artificial surfaces to be used for their sports, but have now moved away from them. The **FA** actually banned their use, although at one time there were several league sides who used them. Now there are none in use for matches. American Football teams found that they were getting a lot of injuries due to hard surfaces and many of the teams are now reverting to grass pitches – although this is obviously not possible for those with indoor stadiums!

Many facilities are benefiting from improved materials used in their construction. Gymnastic areas are now usually purpose-built with sunken areas filled with protective materials. Indoor tennis halls are far more common. Weight-training and lifting equipment is now purpose-built and designed, often with in-built computers that can assist the performers in their training.

Training aids

Improved technology has led to many developments in this area. Computers can now be used in a variety of ways, ranging from monitoring performance to simulating events. Many formula one Grand Prix drivers actually use computerized driving simulators to 'test drive' racing circuits before they actually go there.

Watches are available which can monitor anything from training zones to heart rates and blood pressure, all of which can be done while the performer is working. Computerized machines can be used to check training levels very accurately and there is little doubt that technology is continuing to advance at a very rapid rate, giving more and more help to the committed sports performer.

Landing areas made from synthetic materials have increased safety levels

Glossary

amateur someone who takes part in sport, or an activity, as a pastime or hobby, rather than for gain. They take part for enjoyment only, do not get paid and usually have a full-time job

Amateur Athletic Association the governing body of athletics

amateur status the classification laid down by the rules of the sport, which dictate whether a player is an amateur or not

androgenic anabolic steroids

apartheid a legal system introduced in South Africa in 19?? which discriminated against black and coloured races and segregated them from the white population, leaving them with almost no rights or opportunities

autobiographies a book written by a person, based on their own true life story

beta2agonists stimulant drugs

blood doping the transfusion of blood to help a performance by increasing the number of oxygen-carrying red blood cells in their system

boldenone an anabolic steroid

boot money one of the names given for illegal payments made to amateurs

boycott refuse to attend an event, as a method of protest

Ceefax a teletext system operated by the BBC

controlled drugs the group of illegal and banned drugs

digital compression inter-active TV where viewers can select their own camera angles

doping classes the categories of drugs which are banned by the IOC

doping control the system which is used by sports officials when carrying out drug-testing on sports performers

FA the Football Association, the ruling body of soccer

FIFA the international body which administers world soccer: the letters stand for *Federation Internationale de Football Associations*

Fosbury flop technique used in high jump, named after its founder

'gentlemen' early cricketers who were wealthy and played the game just for fun and enjoyment

Grand Slam the major events in the tennis championships throughout the world

harpaston An ancient Greek game from which football may have developed

hat trick an expression first used in cricket if a bowler got three wickets in succession, now used in many sports for 'three in a row' achievements

hurling an Irish game similar to hockey

IOC the International Olympic Committee, the governing body in charge of the Olympic Games

ISO the Independent Sampling Officer, present at drug-testing of sports performers

journalist someone who makes a living by finding out about events or people and writing articles for newspapers or magazines

lawn tennis full name for the game of tennis which developed from real tennis

listed events protected sporting events which, by government legislation, can only be shown on terrestrial television

locker room interviews arrangement whereby players are interviewed immediately after sporting events, often in the changing area

martial arts combat sports or methods of self defence, usually of oriental origin

MCC the Marylebone Cricket Club, the ruling body of cricket

nandrolone a compound with tissue building function

NFL the National Football League, the governing body of American Football

open sport events or competitions which are open for both amateurs and professionals to play in together

pay per view certain sporting events which can only be seen on satellite networks if the viewer pays an extra fee

performance-enhancing drugs drugs taken by a sportsperson to improve their performance

'players' early professional cricketers who were paid to play

press conference a meeting at which information is given to journalists

professional someone who takes part in sport, or an activity, as a means of earning their livelihood; they get paid for taking part and do it as a full-time job

propaganda exercise an event where misleading and biased information is given out for political purposes

real tennis a form of tennis first played in the Middle Ages

rebel tours sporting tours arranged by the South African authorities who invited leading sports performers to their country, even though they were banned by the sports ruling bodies

semi-professional someone who has a job and also takes part in sport, for which they are legally paid

shamateur people who claim to be amateurs but are in fact being paid to take part, usually with illegal payments

shinty an Irish game similar to hockey

side effects the unwanted, and often harmful, effects which drugs can have on the user

social drugs drugs taken by people for social reasons, for pleasure or exhilaration

sphairistike an ancient Greek game similar to tennis

stanozolol an anabolic agent

steroids chemical compounds similar to the male hormone, testosterone

Superbowl the climax of the American football season when the two most successful teams meet in the final game

Teletext information, broadcast as printed text on TV

terrestrial television the TV stations which broadcast to all homes without using a satellite

test match the name given to an international match, usually in rugby or cricket

testosterone hormone which produces male characteristics

third umpire an extra official in cricket who makes decisions after watching television replays

training drugs performance-enhancing drugs which allow the performer to train longer and harder

weigh-in being weighed before or after competitive sports in which weight is a qualifying factor

World Cup the name for the international championship, usually the soccer world cup, although there are now world cup competitions in other sports

Index